The late George Watts, one of the last of the hand blade forgers in Sheffield, in his workshop at the Kelham Island Industrial Museum making a large bowie blade.

THE CUTLERY INDUSTRY

Peter Smithurst

CONTENTS

Set in 9 point Times roman and printed in Great Britain by C. I. Thomas & Sons (Haverfordwest) Ltd, Press Buildings, Merlins Bridge, Haverfordwest, Dyfed.

British Library Cataloguing in Publication Data available.

The Lancashire Library
ROSSENDALE

ACKNOWLEDGEMENTS

Illustrations are acknowledged as follows: Ernest Benn and Company, page 8 (lower); Graham Clayton, page 29 (bottom); Cutlers Company, Sheffield, page 6; Cadbury Lamb, page 4; Stanley Tools Limited, page 26 (lower); Taylor's Eye Witness, Sheffield, page 12; Worshipful Company of Cutlers of London, page 3. All other illustrations are from the collections of Sheffield City Museums and special thanks are due to the Director of Museums for permission to draw extensively upon this material and to Molly Pearce and David Sier for providing photographs of items within the cutlery collections. Thanks are also due to Graham Clayton and Rowland Swinden for making their time and experience so freely available.

COVER: *Detail from 'The Two Grinders' by Godfrey Sykes (1825-66). The grinding of blades for knives exposed the craftsmen not only to the danger of bursting grindstones but also to the inevitability of painful and fatal disease resulting from the continual inhalation of steel and stone dust.*

02802672

BELOW: *Cutlery from the seventeenth and eighteenth centuries. (From the top.) One of a pair of wedding knives, made in London in 1633, with ivory and amber handle. A London-made knife of the late seventeenth century having an ivory handle with inlays of silver and coloured composition. A mid eighteenth-century Sheffield knife with Staffordshire salt-glazed stoneware handle. Another Sheffield knife of the same period having bone scales decorated with horn inlay.*

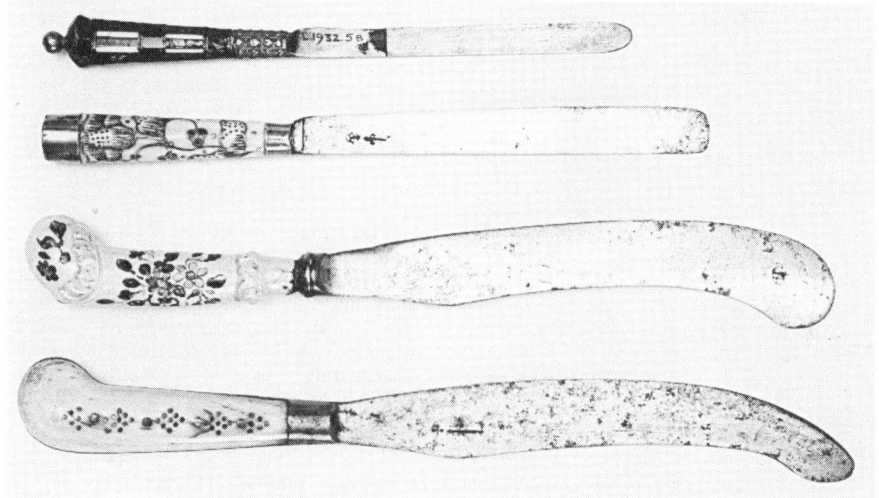

Detail from Creswick's terra cotta frieze adorning the Cutlers' Hall in London.

HISTORY OF THE INDUSTRY

The terms 'cutlery' and 'cutler' are probably derived from the Latin words *cultellus*, meaning a knife, and *cultellarius*, a knife maker, and the cutlery industry was originally concerned only with knives, but over the years the industry and our conception of cutlery has gradually grown to include such other items as razors, scissors, forks and spoons. This book is not a history of these products but of the industry which produced them, although as its recorded history dates back to the twelfth century, it is possible to give only the general outlines.

To our distant forebears a knife was an essential implement, whether it was used as a weapon, a tool or simply for eating with. Most smiths would probably sometimes be called upon to make a knife of some form. For many it would remain an occasional diversion from their normal business. For others it would become a full-time occupation, and a new trade, that of the cutler, was established. It is impossible to say exactly when and where this happened. Cutlery making existed as a separate trade in London in the twelfth century and the earliest name associated with this trade is that of 'Adam the Cutler'. Even by the early thirteenth century the cutlers of London were sufficiently numerous to have formed themselves into a guild to control all aspects of the trade.

The power and importance of the London cutlery trade grew and over the next six hundred years five cutlers' halls were built. The most recent one, close to St Paul's Cathedral, was built in 1886. By this time, however, London had been eclipsed by Sheffield as the centre of the industry.

The monopoly of the London cutlers had long been threatened, however. In the fourteenth and fifteenth centuries they had complained of goods made in 'divers parts of the Kingdom', and falsely marked, being sold in the city. These 'divers parts' were not specified but we know that within this period a distinct cutlery trade existed in a variety of places, such as Thaxted in Essex, Ferry Fryston near Pontefract in West Yorkshire, Leicester, Ashbourne in Derby-

The fine hall of the Cutlers' Guild at Thaxted, Essex.

shire, Salisbury, York and Birmingham. Of these only Salisbury and Birmingham achieved a lasting importance. The reputation of Salisbury rested upon scissors and spring knives and lasted well into the nineteenth century, though by this time the quantities produced were small. The trade in Birmingham, on the other hand, built its reputation on a very specialised branch of cutlery, swordmaking, and remained important in this respect until recent times.

For the rest, however, the trade disappeared without trace, save in the odd instance where it is commemorated in a name, such as Knifesmithgate in Chesterfield and Knifesmith Street in Bristol, or by a building such as the magnificent guildhall at Thaxted. It is at this time too that the first known reference to Sheffield cutlery was made, in an inventory of King Edward III's possessions in the Tower of London in 1340. A few years later Chaucer mentioned a 'Sheffield thwyttle' (a crude general-purpose knife) in his *Canterbury Tales*. Despite such references, however, the trade in Sheffield was neither large nor important. The records of a poll tax levied in 1379 show that while there were a few cutlers working in the neighbourhood of Sheffield, there were none in Sheffield itself. Over the next two hundred years this situation was to change remarkably.

THE RISE OF SHEFFIELD

In 1575 George Talbot, Earl of Shrewsbury, Lord of the Manor of Sheffield, husband of Bess of Hardwick and custodian of Mary Queen of Scots, sent a case of Sheffield knives to Lord Burghley, describing them as 'such things as my poor country affordeth with fame throughout the realm'. A few years later the author of *The Writing Schoolmaster* recommends 'first then be your choice of penknife! A right Sheffield knife is best'. Sheffield cutlery was even being exported abroad. By this time the Sheffield cutlers operated under a guild system with the Lord of the Manor at its head but when his successor died in 1617 the guild system came to an end also. The trade in Sheffield fell into complete disarray in the absence of authority. So alarmed did the established cutlers become that in 1621 a bill was presented before Parliament seeking consent to the formation of a new controlling body. Three years later the bill received consent and became an

Act of Parliament 'for the good order and government of the makers of knives, sickles, shears, scissors and other cutlery wares in Hallamshire'. Under this Act, the Company of Cutlers in Hallamshire was formed, two hundred years after its London counterpart. Hallamshire was a region surrounding the Sheffield of 1624, its area roughly corresponding with the present city boundaries. The present Cutlers' Hall testifies both to the prestige of the company and to the trade it represents and it houses some fine examples of the cutler's art. Although the company lost most of its authority in the early nineteenth century it still retains some important functions and the title of Master Cutler is deemed a great honour. The investiture of the holder at the Cutlers' Feast remains a significant annual occasion in Sheffield.

When the company was formed there were around five hundred names on the register and the Sheffield cutlery trade had outstripped all rivals except London and possibly York.

There were two factors which had a significant effect on this early development of the industry in Sheffield. One was the abundance of a local sandstone

from which grindstones used by the cutlers were made. Its quality was so good that grindstones made from it were exported to Europe. The second and more important factor was the availability of water power. Sheffield is situated at the confluence of five fast-flowing rivers which rise in the nearby hills. When someone, possibly in the late middle ages, had the idea of using water power to turn the grindstones of the cutlers and toolmakers, Sheffield was ideally placed to take full advantage of this new technology. By the time the Cutlers' Company was formed there were 28 cutlers' *wheels* (workshops for grinding cutlery and edge tools) around the town. This gave Sheffield a great advantage over all other cutlery manufacturing areas which was exploited even more extensively in succeeding years. By the 1770s the number of water-powered workshops had increased to over 150, all within about 5 miles (8 km) of the town centre.

Throughout the seventeenth and early eighteenth centuries the cutlery trade in Sheffield continued to grow. Then, in the middle of the eighteenth century it received a new impetus. Around 1742 Benjamin Huntsman, working in Shef-

The present Cutlers' Hall in Sheffield as illustrated in a special supplement to The Graphic in 1874. It was built in 1832 at a cost of £6500.

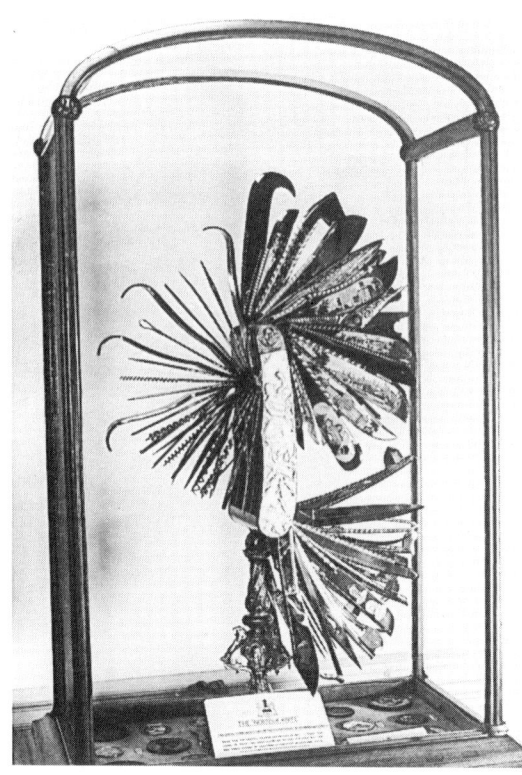

field, produced a revolutionary new material, crucible steel. Huntsman was a maker of watches and clocks and it is possible that he had difficulty in making the delicate components of watches from *blister steel*, the only steel available at the time, which was made as an extension of the process of making wrought iron. Wrought iron was made by heating pig iron and subjecting it to a blast of air in a furnace known as a *finery*. Gradually the hard brittle lumps of iron were transformed into a red hot spongy mass containing a molten slag formed from the impurities present. The iron sponge was then gathered into a ball on the end of an iron pole, removed from the furnace and shaped under a hammer into a bar. Most of the slag was squeezed out in the process but not all. Some remained as thin streaks, invisible to the naked eye. These bars of iron were then used to make blister steel by packing them in charcoal and baking at red heat for

several days in a *cementation* or *converting furnace*. The iron absorbed carbon, acquiring in the process a blistered surface, and was converted into blister steel. This steel, because it had never been molten, still retained the streaks of slag present in the original iron. Also the absorption of carbon was rarely uniform and might vary considerably within a single bar. To minimise some of these defects, *shear steel* was often made by piling several short bars of blister steel into a *faggot,* heating in the hearth and welding together under the water-powered tilt hammer. For even better quality, the process could be repeated on the shear steel to produce *double shear steel.*

However, even this was not good enough for Huntsman, who wanted absolute purity and uniformity. To achieve this he developed the simple method of melting blister steel in crucibles, skimming off the slag, which floated to the

Brincliffe Edge quarry, one of several in and around Sheffield producing grindstones for the cutlery and edge-tool trades.

surface, and pouring the liquid steel into a mould to solidify. The result was an ingot of *crucible* or *cast steel*. It was far superior to anything else available at the time and, once this was appreciated, its use became widespread. Initially the Sheffield cutlers rejected it, claiming it was too difficult to work. Crucible steel was used by the French cutlers, however, and the Sheffield cutlers, seeing their reputation and market at risk, petitioned Parliament to prohibit its export. Fortunately Parliament refused and the cutlers of Sheffield were forced to use crucible steel, which became a mark of quality in cutlery and tools for almost two hundred years.

THE 'LITTLE MESTERS'

There was a reorganisation of the industry in the eighteenth century. In the early days a cutler made a knife from start to finish and found his own market. The trade had grown to such a degree by the late eighteenth century and the products had become so diverse that this

Shepherd Wheel, Sheffield. Dating from at least 1584, this is probably the oldest surviving water-powered workshop for the grinding of edge tools and cutlery in Britain. Its protection from demolition in the 1930s was largely due to the efforts of the Sheffield Trades Historical Society and the Council for the Conservation of Sheffield's Antiquities. The restoration work was continued by the City Council's Museums Department. It was opened to the public in 1975.

approach was no longer practical. Specialisation had become necessary, not just in the manufacture of a particular class of knife such as butcher knives, table knives, pen and pocket knives, shoe knives and so on, but also in the various stages of their manufacture. Thus the manufacture of a knife was now being

ABOVE: *An early Sheffield steelworks. The conical building is the cementation or converting furnace in which the blister steel was produced. The artist, W. Botham, is thought to have worked in Sheffield only during 1802-4.*
BELOW: *Shear steel continued to be made by the same process well into the twentieth century although the steam hammer had long replaced water-powered hammers. Here blister steel bars are piled into a 'faggot' for welding together.*

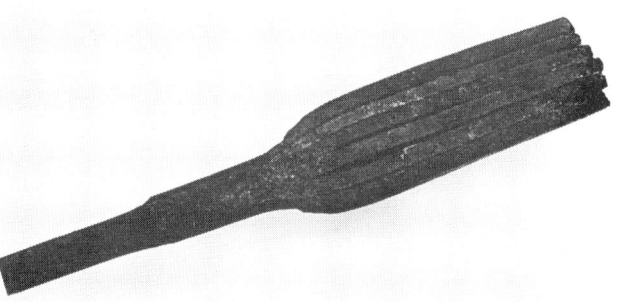

Shear steel in the making, showing how the bars of blister steel become welded into a single bar, or 'string', of shear steel.

carried out by, principally, three separate craftsmen: the *forger*, who fashioned the blade; the *grinder*, who gave it its lustre and an edge; and the *cutler*, who finished it and fitted it with some form of handle. These craftsmen's titles were therefore very specific, such as table-blade forger, butcher-knife grinder, pen and pocket knife cutler.

The manufacturing operations now needed co-ordination and this was achieved in two ways. Some cutlers, with sufficient working capital, were able to commission work from forgers and grinders, finish the items themselves and sell them. Also, some outsiders, with no practical experience of the trade but having the necessary finances, bought in

The final step in making crucible steel is 'teeming' the molten steel into a mould. It was a very skilled job, requiring both strength and delicacy to pour 60 pounds (27 kg) or more of steel into a narrow mould without the stream of steel touching the sides. Note the wet sacking around the legs and forearms of the 'teemer' to protect him from the searing heat.

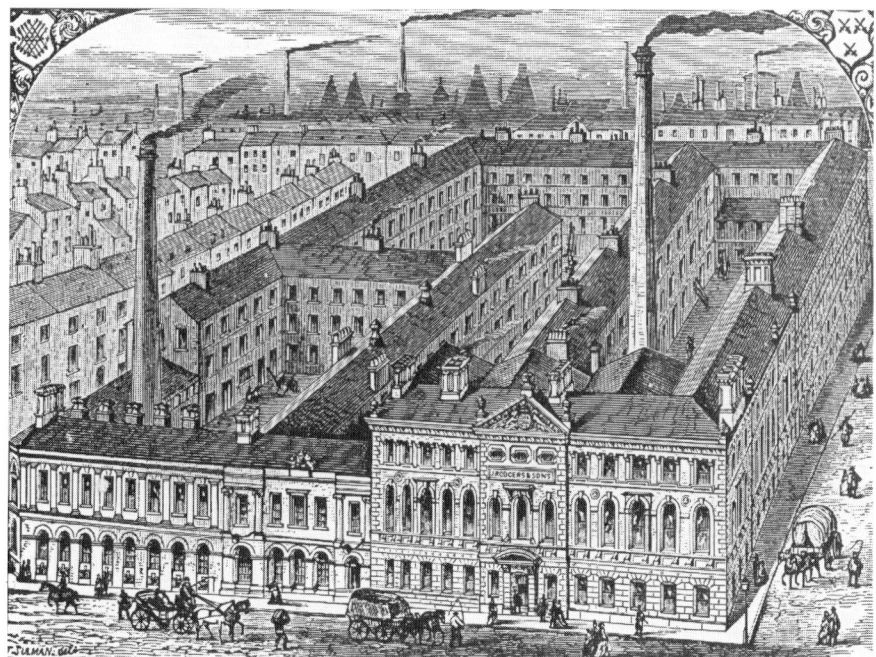

The Norfolk Street premises of Joseph Rodgers and Sons in Sheffield in 1862 was perhaps the best known name in cutlery in the nineteenth and early twentieth centuries. Like most of their contemporaries Rodgers made all types of cutlery but they are probably best remembered for their spring knives.

all the craftsmanship and sold the products under their own name. These people were known as *factors*.

By the mid nineteenth century many of the cutlers who had followed this course had become leading names in the industry. They built large factories, often with lavish showrooms in which to display their goods, to satisfy the ever increasing demands of their worldwide markets. In the nineteenth century the cutlery industry in Sheffield became enormous. In 1841 the number of people engaged in the trade in Sheffield was almost ten thousand, whereas in London it was one thousand. Fifty years later the figure for Sheffield had risen by half again whilst that for London had been halved.

The change in the organisation of the industry brought about another division, not in labour but in status. The large firms, the big masters, rarely employed direct labour but farmed out work to hundreds of self-employed craftsmen, who employed perhaps one or two hands

and became known as *Little Mesters*. It was, perhaps, a unique way of operating a large industry. A Little Mester might rent workshop space in one company's factory yet be free to do work for another. This system gave the companies great flexibility, being able to satisfy almost any specialist demand without massive overheads. The craftsmen had the flexibility to work for whoever they chose and were not at the mercy of one company's fortunes. This system prevailed until the Second World War, after which it declined in the face of mechanisation. Now there are only a few Little Mesters, two of whom can be seen in their workshops at the Kelham Island Industrial Museum, Sheffield, where they carry out their business and perpetuate a centuries-old tradition.

MODERN TIMES

In 1913 Harry Brearley, a metallurgist at Thomas Firth and Sons in Sheffield, produced a steel which did not rust.

LEFT: *Examples of nineteenth-century trade labels. A manufacturer's pride extended even to such mundane items as these.*

RIGHT: *Harry Brearley, the Sheffield metallurgist who invented stainless steel.*

11

Stainless steel was very different from ordinary steel and the cutlers at first claimed that it was too difficult to forge or could not be hardened and tempered properly. Many cutlers tried to use it and failed and Brearley was dubbed 'the inventor of knives that won't cut', but he persevered and by the 1920s stainless cutlery began to appear on the market and the days of ordinary carbon steel were numbered. However, knives made of carbon steel, the modern equivalent of crucible steel, can still be obtained and are thought by some to hold a better edge.

The cutlery trade, like most other manufacturing industries in Britain, was hit by serious recessions during the 1970s and 1980s, caused by various factors, not the least of which was cheap foreign imports, but Sheffield cutlery is unsurpassed in quality and alongside the traditional patterns are to be found such items as Kitchen Devils and Laser Knives. The future of the industry depends on the customer and remains uncertain so long as the quality of the product is considered less important than its price.

If you have a knife marked 'double shear' or 'warranted cast steel' or 'Firth-Brearley stainless' it represents a milestone in metallurgical history and in the development of the skills of the craftsmen who made it. If you want a knife that will become a family heirloom, look for one marked 'made in Sheffield'.

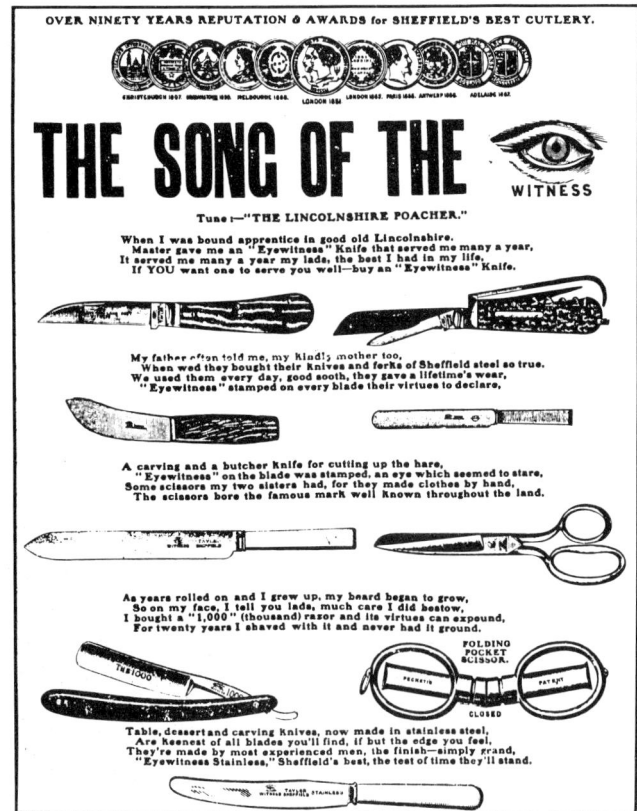

An unusual piece of manufacturers' publicity material from the early days of the stainless steel era.

The table-blade grinder's 'hull': an engraving from the Illustrated London News of 1866 showing a typical interior of the period. Note the 'hack hammer', used for truing up the grindstone, resting on the squatting board of the grinder in the foreground.

MANUFACTURING PROCESSES

Because of the great range and variety of knives produced by the cutlery industry it would be impossible, in this book, to describe the manufacturing processes of them all. The familiar table knife and the pen or pocket knife have therefore been selected as representative examples. The processes used in their manufacture apply in principle to other types of cutlery and serve to give a good overall idea of production methods. This section has also been restricted to cover the traditional methods of manufacture, where the skill of the craftsman was dominant. The processes may seem archaic, as indeed they are, but mechanisation is relatively recent and even now some of the hand skills remain because the machine does not have the same instant adaptability or versatility.

FORGING

The first stage in the making of any blade is forging, whereby a piece of hot steel is hammered into the desired shape. Traditionally this was done entirely by hand and the needs of the hand forger were few: a workshop, perhaps no more than 10 feet (3 metres) square, containing a hearth, bellows, stithy (anvil), hammers and tongs and a few very simple but specialised tools, depending upon the type of blades being forged. Often the workshop would be in the forger's own backyard. Alternatively it might have been rented in one of the large tenement workshops or factories which began to appear in Sheffield from the late eighteenth century onwards.

The hand forging of a penknife or pocket-knife blade, for instance, was a *single-handed* or one-man operation and could be divided into three distinct stages. The first was *mooding*, in which a bar of steel, or *string*, of appropriate width and thickness for the blade being made, was taken and one end of it was forged down to the approximate shape and size. This part-formed blade is called a *mood*.

While still hot, the mood was cut from the string by laying on a chisel, or *agon*, set up on the stithy and striking it with the hammer. The cut end was then reheated in the hearth and the *tang* forged. The tang is the portion of a blade by which it is secured to, or forms part of, its handle and this stage of the process was called *tanging*.

Smithing was the final stage, in which the blade was brought to its finished forged state, principally by completing the thinning-out process to form what was to become the cutting edge. It was also usually the stage at which the *nail nick* was put in, using another special tool set up on the stithy, and the tang was stamped with the name of the 'maker' (the person who sold the finished knife). Sometimes the forger also formed the *choil* during smithing though this was often done at the mooding stage.

In contrast, the hand forging of a table-knife blade was generally a two-handed process, carried out by the forger and an assistant, known as a *striker* or *butty*, who wielded a heavy long-hafted hammer. The process can also be divided into stages similar to those in the forging of penknife and pocket-knife blades but there were distinct differences.

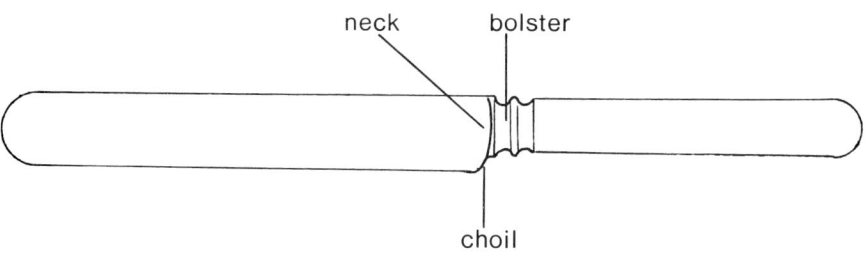

ABOVE: *The main features of a table knife.*
BELOW: *The main features and components of a pen or pocket knife.*

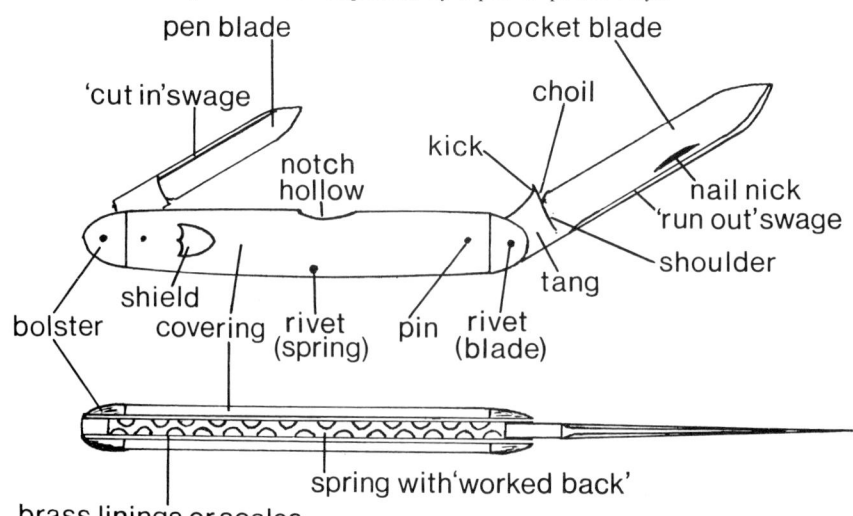

RIGHT: *Stages in the hand forging of a penknife or pocket-knife blade: (from the top) portion of the 'string' or steel bar; the 'mood'; 'tanged' blade; 'smithed' blade. Note that the small 'neb' projecting from the tang was formed simply to give the forger something to grip. It was removed before or during grinding.*

BELOW: *Stages in the forging of a table-knife blade: (from the top) part of the 'string'; the rough forged blade (left) and piece of wrought iron (right); blade and iron welded together; bolster formed; finished 'smithed' blade with all the wrinkles removed.*

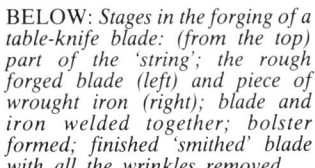

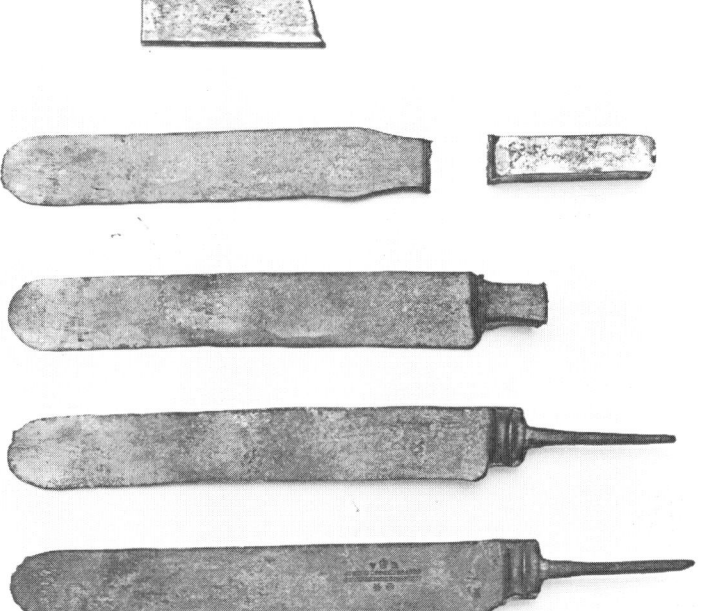

The first stage was also the production of a mood from a bar of steel. Because table-knife blades are long and thin, they required more forging than a pocket-knife blade and this could be carried out much more quickly by two men, avoiding the need for frequent reheating, which could spoil the quality of the steel.

Only the blade portion of a table knife was made of steel. The tang and *bolster* were of iron and before these parts could be formed the mood had to be joined to a piece of wrought iron. This was done by *hammer welding*. The cut end of the

ABOVE: *Pages from a manufacturer's catalogue of about 1920 showing some of the range of knives produced.*

RIGHT: *Two-handed forging of table-knife blades.*

RIGHT: *A pair of 'bolster prints' used to form the bolsters on table-knife blades. The handle for the top print is made from a fresh hazel wand wrapped around it and bound with string, a very common practice in the past.*

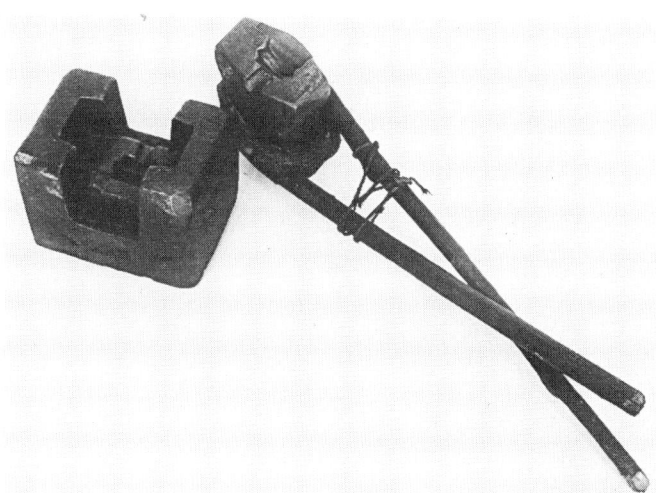

BELOW: *Rowland Swinden, one of the few hand grinders left, today works on a wide range of blades. He is one of the 'Little Mesters' who carry on their business at the Kelham Island Industrial Museum in Sheffield and is seen here using a 'flatstick' to assist him in the grinding of a pocket-knife blade.*

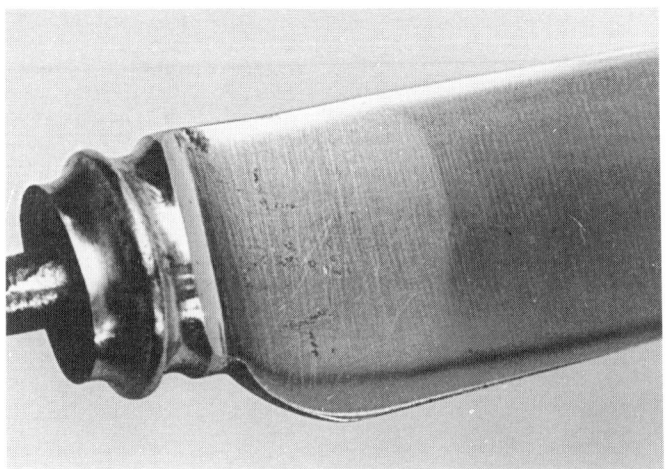

mood and the end of a bar of iron would be brought up to welding heat in the hearth. They were then removed, laid on the anvil with the heated ends overlapping slightly and welded together by hammering. The temperature at which this could take place was critical and the hand forger had no optical pyrometers or thermocouples to aid him. He had to rely solely upon his experience and he rarely made a mistake. The surplus iron was then cut off, leaving exactly the right amount to form the tang and the bolster. This weld is often visible, at the 'neck' on the reverse of table-knife blades made in this way, as a faint mark, similar to a thumb print. For this reason, it is known as the *thumbmark*.

The bolster was formed using a pair of matching dies or *bolster prints*. The prints had cavities cut out of their mating surfaces, corresponding to the shape of bolster required. The bottom print was placed on the anvil and the top print held in tongs by the forger. The heated iron portion of the blade was then placed between the two prints and the top print was hammered by the striker until the bolster had been correctly formed. The small surplus spigot of iron left protruding from the end of the bolster was then heated and drawn out under the hammer to produce the tang.

In its final stage the process followed the same pattern as for penknife and pocket-knife blades. For table knives smithing was principally the flattening and straightening of the long thin blades which would by this time have acquired a few twists and bends.

Whatever the type of blade being produced, the skilled forger, working by hand and eye alone, could make dozens of blade forgings of the same pattern within such close dimensional tolerances that a micrometer would be needed to detect the differences.

HARDENING AND TEMPERING

The forging of the blades was now finished but they were still not ready for grinding. Before this could be carried out they had to be *hardened* and *tempered*. For both hardening and tempering the blade had to be heated to a predetermined temperature, depending upon the steel being used and the properties required of the finished blade, and then cooled.

For hardening, quite high temperatures, about 600 to 900C (1100 to 1650F), were required and the blades were cooled rapidly by *quenching* in oil or a mixture of oil and water. It was essential that the blades were quenched vertically to avoid distortion, especially with the long and thin table blades. The blades were now very hard and brittle and had to be tempered to remove some of the brittleness. This was done by heating the blades slowly to a much lower temperature, about 250 to 300 C (480 to 570 F), and quenching again. The blades remained hard and continued to hold a cutting edge but they became a little more flexible.

These heat treatment processes are now carried out semi-automatically, using thermostatically controlled furnaces that ensure the accuracy of the temperature. In the past temperature control depended entirely upon the skilled eye of the hand forger. When steel is heated it undergoes a series of colour changes beginning with a 'yellowish white' at around 200 C (390 F) and becoming 'white hot' at about 1200 C (2190 F). Between these two extremes it passes through nearly all the colours of the rainbow and from these the skilled forger was able to gauge the temperature of his steel very accurately. Not all the colour changes are apparent to the untrained eye. The layman would probably find it very difficult to distinguish between 'blood red' and 'dark cherry' but to the forger it meant the difference between 650 and 700 C (1220 and 1290 F). At the lower end of the thermometer the *tempering colours* are much more susceptible to changes in temperature (the difference between 'straw' and 'yellow' or 'cornflower blue' and 'light blue' is only 10 degrees) and were further complicated by the fact that the steel was already black from the hardening process.

For this reason, tempering was probably the most difficult of the two processes for the forger. If overheated only slightly the blade could be spoilt and become a *waster*, and the forger took pains to make sure this did not happen. The blades were heated very slowly, often by drawing them repeatedly across a red-hot bar of iron or steel, and were then quenched immediately the correct colour showed.

GRINDING

After hardening and tempering the blades were ready for the next stage in the manufacturing process, grinding. The job of the grinder was to transform the blade forging into the finely finished item ready for assembly by the cutler. Like the forger, the grinder also specialised in one class of blade and his most essential piece of equipment, the grindstone, reflected this. The size of stone varied with the type of work being done and in Sheffield there was a tradition of grinders selling their stones, when they had become too small for their particular purpose, to the next grinder down the line. Thus when a table grinder had worked his stone out he

The basic equipment of the hand grinder and its terminology.

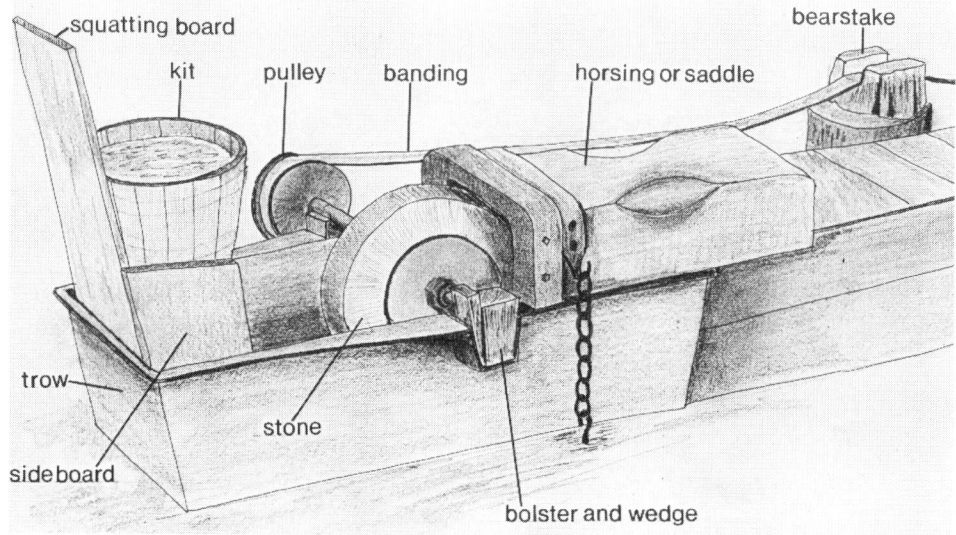

would perhaps pass it on to a penknife and pocket-knife grinder and when he finished with it he might pass it on to a scissor grinder, or even a razor grinder if it was small enough.

The basic equipment of the hand grinder was used until recent times for all blades. Hand grinders are still needed to carry out the work on small orders or special items which are beyond the scope of the machine, although their numbers are much reduced. Their work was carried out in one of the *wheels* (grinding workshops), driven in the early days by water power and later by steam, where they would rent a *trow* (workspace) in one of the *hulls* (workrooms).

The process was carried out in several stages using successively finer abrasives but only the first stage was actually called 'grinding'. This was *rough grinding*, during which the blades were ground all over to remove the hammer marks and scale produced during forging and to give them the correct contour. The grinder performed this task sitting astride his stone on a *horsing* consisting of a *saddle*, usually a large block of oak, crudely shaped and often padded with old sacking for comfort, supported on a wooden framework. The saddle was fitted at the front, and sometimes at the rear, with large iron straps which passed along the top and down the sides, terminating in hooks. These hooks were connected to heavy chains which were used to anchor the whole assembly to the floor. This was necessary to prevent the grinder and his horsing being thrown into the air if his stone burst at high speed and a large fragment struck the underside of his saddle. A penknife-blade grinder's stone was perhaps 6 inches (15 cm) wide and 2 feet 6 inches (76 cm) in diameter and rotated at 300 to 600 revolutions per minute, giving a peripheral speed of between 2400 and 4700 feet per minute (25-53 mph, 40-84 km/h), so its fracture was a potential source of danger.

The French cutlery grinders at Thiers usually carried out their work lying face down on a board and most illustrations of them show a small pet dog lying across the backs of their ankles. It is supposed by some that the dog was able to sense the impending fracture of a stone and when it removed itself it gave warning to the grinder to do likewise.

There were two principal causes of stones bursting. One was the presence of flaws in the natural sandstone from which the grindstones were made and the grinder had to check his stone very carefully before and during use. The second cause was an unbalanced stone and the grinder had to take special care that when he had finished hanging the stone on its spindle it ran true. He might also find that during use the stone wore unevenly and ran out of true. This would be corrected by careful use of the *hack hammer,* an adze-like tool, to chip away the high spots on the face of the stone.

The stone ran in a *trow,* a metal tank or trough set in the floor and containing water. The water level was continually adjusted during work so that it just touched the bottom of the stone, which was therefore kept permanently wet. The water prevented the blades from becoming overheated, or *burnt,* during grinding and having their temper spoilt. It also helped to prevent the formation of dust. Instead, the fine particles of stone and steel produced were thrown off the stone as a yellowish sludge known as *wheelswarf.* Most of the stone was encased by the trow and the horsing and these became encrusted with swarf. The wheelswarf thrown forward off the stone was caught on a short plank or *squatting board* standing on end in front of the trow. If the grinder had to stop his stone for any reason and leave it for longer than a few moments, he would always ladle some water out of the trow back into his *kitt* so that the stone would not soak up water on its bottom side and become out of balance.

One end of the spindle which carried the stone was fitted with a wooden pulley to take the flat leather belt or *band* which connected it with a countershaft running along the rear of the hull and provided the motive power. Leather belts tended to stretch slightly and to maintain the tension a large block of wood, known as a *bearstake,* was propped up underneath the top belt. These bearstakes after long use had beautifully polished deep grooves worn in them.

After rough grinding came *whittening,*

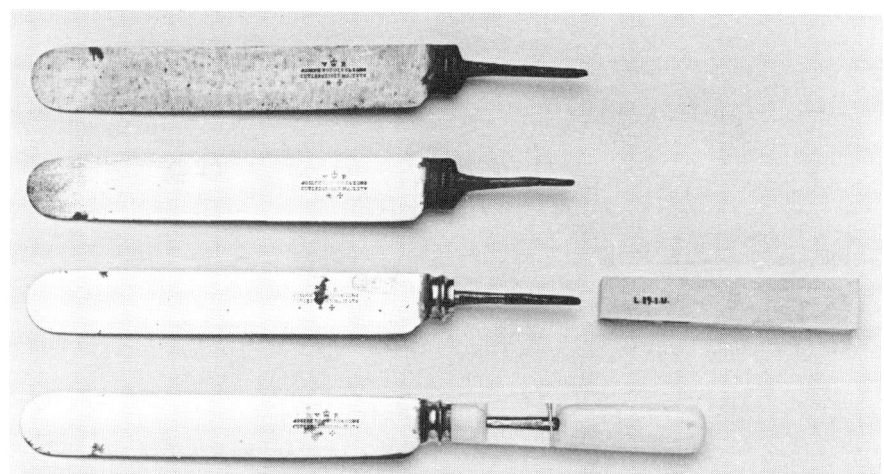

Various stages in the grinding of a blade: (from the top) rough ground blade; rough glazed blade; polished blade; a finished knife sectioned to display one method of fitting the handle.

which was carried out on a fine-grained, hard stone. This stage allowed the grinder to correct any slight deviation in size or shape of the blade and removed the marks left by rough grinding. It was the last stage in which a grindstone was used. The remaining three stages, which were all designed to give the blade its flawless finish, were carried out using wooden wheels. These were built up in segments, like the slices of a cake, and were fitted with leather rims, the rim and wheel being around 1½ inches (38 mm) wide. The first two of these final stages were known as *rough glazing* and *fine glazing* and were carried out on *glazing wheels*, or *glazers* as they were generally called. The wheels were prepared for use, or *dressed*, by having their leather rims coated with glue and then being rolled in abrasive powder.

Glazing produced blades which were smooth and bright but were still not quite finished. Their final lustre and brilliance were given in the last of the operations carried out by the grinder, *buffing*. The *buff* was a wooden wheel similar to the glazer but it traditionally had a rim made up of buffalo leather — hence its name. Since buffalo leather was not a common material it was often replaced by leather from the neck of a bull. The finest finish

was achieved with rouge, usually known as *crocus powder*, a very fine iron oxide, and a crocus-polished blade has a quality of its own, rarely achieved today.

Of all the cutlery grinding trades pen and pocket blade grinding were probably the most skilled. All followed a similar pattern except that trade knives (shoe, butchers', farriers' and other tool-like knives) were not given such a high finish. The table-knife grinder had to work to very close tolerances to produce sets of blades which matched in size and finish. The trade which differed most from the others was razor grinding. The old-fashioned open or cut-throat razors are deeply *hollow ground*, that is to say, the side of the blade is hollowed out from edge to back. This was achieved using very small stones, 4 inches (100 mm) or even less in diameter, the curvature of the hollow grinding matching the curvature of the stone. Most grinders, however, were aiming for a perfectly flat or even slightly convex surface and it was very difficult to achieve this on a round stone, which would naturally produce a hollow. The usual method was to use a *flatstick*, a simple piece of wood shaped to fit a particular type or size of blade on one side, the other side being left exposed for grinding. This was one of the

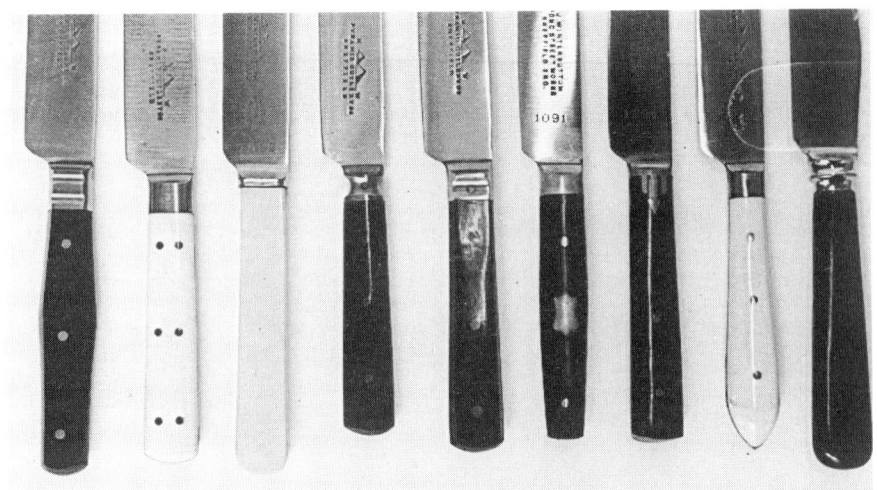

A few of the different styles and materials used in the handles of table knives in the early twentieth century.

very few tools the grinder used and enabled him to control the blade and exert an even pressure on it in contact with the stone.

THE TABLE-KNIFE CUTLER

The third and final stage in the making of a knife is the fitting of the blade to some form of handle, and it is to the craftsman carrying out this work that the term 'cutler' is specifically applied today. There was more work and skill in this task than the basic definition of the job suggests.

Although the table knife only consists of two principal components, the blade and the handle, the cutlery trade created a great diversity. Changes in the pattern of blade or bolster were limited but gave some flexibility. The greatest variety occurs in the style and materials of the handle. Handles could be severely plain or highly ornamental. They could be made from a wide range of material: rosewood, ebony, beech, horn, stag, bone, ivory, mother-of-pearl, porcelain, silver, gold. The supply and rough preparation of these materials to the cutlery trade constituted an industry in itself with specialist pearl, bone and ivory cutters, horn pressers and so on. In the mid

nineteenth century there were almost 150 firms in Sheffield carrying out this aspect of the business alone. It is estimated that in 1887 72,000 stag handles and scales were produced weekly for the spring-knife and table-knife trades. Vast quantities of ivory were used, one Sheffield supplier having 122 tons in stock at a time, with sales of about £6000 monthly. Cheaper than ivory or stag was the black horn from the American buffalo and it was consumed in truckloads, even in the early twentieth century.

The first synthetic substitute for ivory, known under various names such as Crayford ivory, Fictile ivory and Xylonite, appeared about 1870. Celluloid was produced around the same time, and these materials soon began to replace the natural ones. In 1947 it was estimated that the Sheffield table-knife cutlers alone used 24 million celluloid handles.

The simplest and cheapest form of table knife was one with a plain wide flat tang, to each side of which were riveted flat pieces of wood known as *scales*. Before fixing, the scales and tang had to be drilled. In the days before machines this was carried out using a *fiddle drill*, a simple device comprising a *breastplate*, a drilling bit, known in Sheffield as a *parser*, and a *boring stick*. The parser was basically a small bar of tool steel, approximately ¼ inch (6 mm) square and 9 inches (230 mm) long. One end was tapered to a point and, during use, this end ran in a bearing formed by a small cavity in the breastplate, a steel plate strapped to the cutler's chest. The opposite end was forged and honed to form a diamond-shaped point with a cutting edge. The rotary motion was given to the parser by means of the boring stick, a thin wooden shaft about 30 inches (760 mm) long with a loose leather thong anchored close to each end. The thong was wrapped once around a wooden bobbin fixed on the shank of the parser, the two ends of the parser were positioned correctly in the breastplate and the object to be drilled, and the drilling operation was performed by moving the boring stick rapidly from side to side. It was essential that the slack leather thong should become taut when wrapped around the bobbin, otherwise it would slip rather than drive the parser. In the hands of an expert this was a very efficient tool and many craftsmen preferred it long after the introduction of 'improved' drilling equipment.

When all the holes had been drilled the knife and scales were ready for riveting together. The rivet was a brass or German silver wire about ¹⁄₁₆ inch (1.5 mm) in diameter, pushed into the hole. A short straight length of this wire was used to secure the scales loosely to the tang and the excess was cut off, leaving a small stub projecting which was hammered flat on the *cutler's stiddy*, a miniature anvil set in the bench top. This process relied upon the wire swelling outwards as a result of the hammering in order to fit very tightly in the hole. The scales could then be filed flush with the edges of the tang in preparation for the final operation to give the handle a smooth and polished finish.

The first stage in this process was *glazing down*, using a wheel similar to the rough glazing wheel of the grinder. This stage was often known as *mousing*, because when carried out on a bone handle it produced a smell reminiscent of mice. Finally the handle was buffed to give a smooth, polished finish.

The components of the fiddle drill, consisting of the breastplate (lower left) and the boring stick (centre) with its leather thong wrapped around the bobbin of the parser.

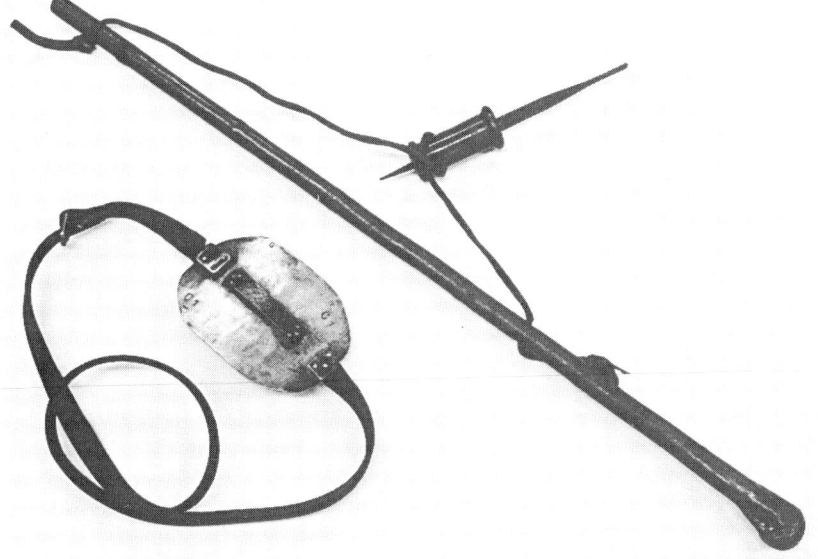

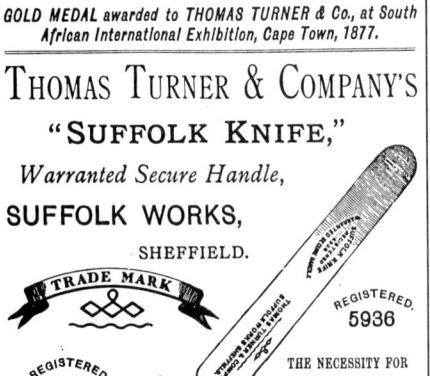

An advertisement which shows one of the methods used for securing the handles of higher-quality table knives.

Other methods were used for fixing the handles of knives of higher quality, which were generally made in one piece rather than two. Such knives usually had a narrow round tang which fitted into a longitudinal hole bored in the handle and was held in place by a mixture of resin and fine ashes. A more sophisticated method was to have the tang passing right through the handle; a small brass washer was fitted to the end and riveted in place. If even more security of fixing was required a cross pin could be fitted which passed laterally through the handle and tang to prevent the handle turning.

THE SPRING-KNIFE CUTLER

A spring knife is much more complicated than a table knife and spring-knife cutlers were, and generally still are,

considered to be the most highly skilled. A spring knife is one in which the blades are held open or closed by means of a spring. Pen and pocket knives, lock knives, folding bowies and the ill-reputed flick knife are all spring knives. It is not known when the first spring knives were made but there is a legend that they were introduced to Sheffield by a cutler named Jacques of Liège who came to England to escape religious persecution in the late seventeenth century, giving rise to the once common nickname for a pocket knife, 'jackaleg', and perhaps to the term 'jack knife'.

There is a distinction between a penknife and a pocket knife. In its original sense a pen knife was used for cutting a quill to the correct shape for writing and for this a very fine and hard blade was required. A pocket knife was a much heavier instrument with a tough blade to withstand rough use. However, the two types of blade were often combined in a single knife and a general distinction was that if the blades were fixed at opposite ends it was a pen knife and if fixed at the same end it was a pocket knife.

Spring knives are subject to great variation, far more than table knives. They have a greater variety of blade styles, each with a range of sizes, and in addition there are other implements which were often included: buttonhooks, corkscrews, gimlets, saws, scissors, reamers, cigar forks, tin openers, bottle openers, nail files, eraser blades, marlin spikes, cartridge extractors, screwdrivers, palette knives and rulers were all often built into spring knives of some form and gave almost endless scope for the spring-knife cutler.

There are several marks of quality to look for in a spring knife. The first is that the blades should operate smoothly against the spring, 'snap' into the open and closed positions and not rub against each other when folded away. Secondly, the blades should not open too far or too little, nor should they close too far, obscuring the nail nick and making the knife impossible to open, nor close too little, leaving the point exposed. Nor must the blades wobble from side to side, a defect known as a *headache*. To meet these criteria, the springs must be of

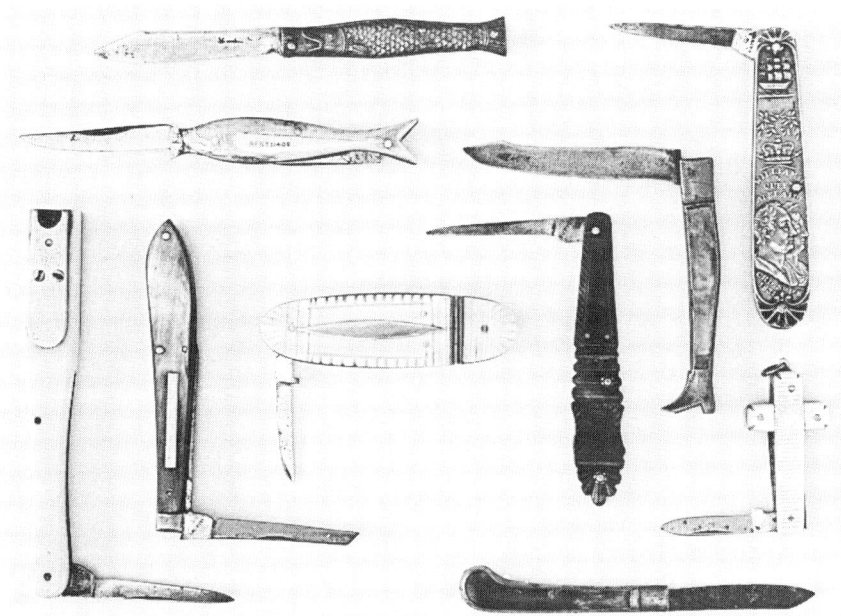

ABOVE: *A group of Sheffield-made penknives, ranging from the late eighteenth century to the late nineteenth century, showing a variety of designs and covering materials.*
BELOW: *A group of Sheffield-made penknives and pocket knives, dating from about 1680 to 1950, showing a range of styles and materials.*

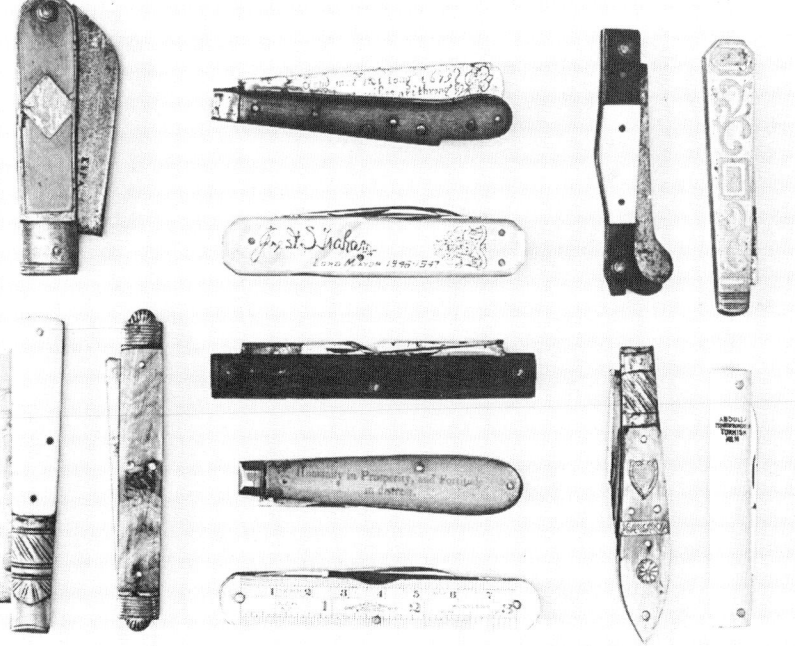

correct length, the tangs of the blades must fit snugly into the ends of the spring and both spring and blades must be in exactly the right relative positions in the finished knife.

In achieving all this, the cutler used some very simple devices. The positioning of the rivet holes in springs and blades was critical and to ensure repeatable accuracy a *marking devil* was used. A different one was needed for each type and size of spring and blade. It consisted of a flat plate fitted with a small projecting hardened steel point and raised shoulders against which the spring or blade was held before being given a sharp blow with a hammer. This left a small dimple in the spring, which served to position the boring tool. When the rivet hole had been bored, the spring was matched up against a hardened dummy

ABOVE: *A superb example of the spring-knife cutler's art. This knife, which measures only 1 inch (25 mm) long when closed, has 61 different implements, each of which functions perfectly. Unfortunately neither the name of the maker nor the date of manufacture is known.*

RIGHT: *This is perhaps the most unusual testament to the spring-knife cutler's skills and craftsmanship ever made, the so called 'Year Knife'. It was made by Joseph Rodgers and Sons for the Great Exhibition of 1851 and contained 1851 blades or implements. Since that date a further blade has been added annually so that when photographed it contained 1986.*

A cutler's 'marking devil', used for marking the positions for the holes in springs.

spring, using a pin through both holes to locate them accurately. The spring and dummy were clamped in a vice and the spring ends filed to match those of the dummy. The same process was applied to the blades, using an appropriate marking devil and a hardened dummy blade, known as a *squaring tang*, to serve as a guide for the filing of the tangs.

To ensure that the blades and springs were correctly positioned in the finished knife, a *boring plate* was used to guide the boring tool in drilling the rivet holes in the *linings* or *webs*, the structural framework of the spring knife. Some-

times the same rivets that held the blades and springs in position were also used to secure the outer *coverings*. In this case the boring plate would serve for the boring of these also, and as a jig for the filing of coverings and webs to shape. On better-quality knives, however, the coverings were riveted, or *pinned on*, separately. At this stage the cutler would probably assemble the knife temporarily to ensure that everything was in order and to allow him to correct any defects that might be apparent. It would then be knocked apart again and he would begin work on the coverings or scales.

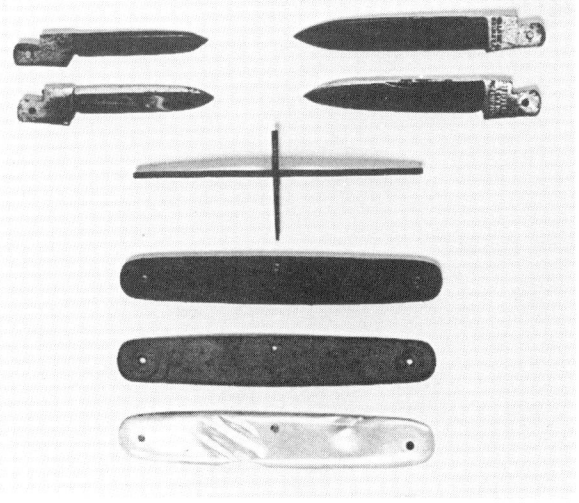

Some of the implements used by the spring-knife cutler: (top left) a 'squaring tang' for a pen blade with the filed blade below it; (top right) a 'squaring tang' for the pocket blade with the filed blade below; (centre) a dummy hardened spring with its locating pin, used for filing the springs to length; (bottom) a 'boring plate' used to guide the drilling of the holes in the linings and coverings shown below it.

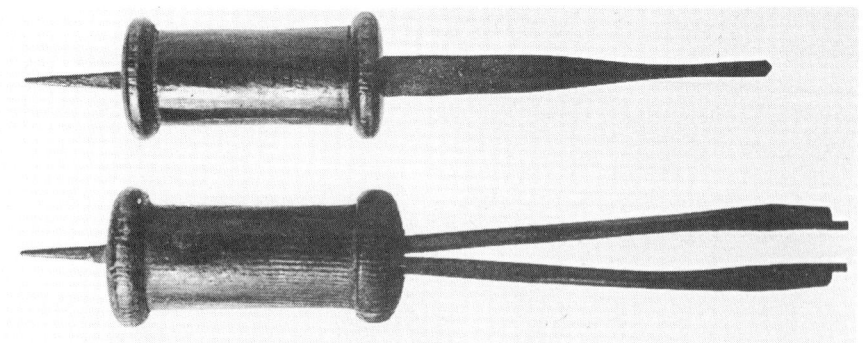

ABOVE: *The two-legged or shielding parser (bottom) compared with the ordinary boring parser (top).*

LEFT: *A selection of shielding plates used in conjunction with the two-legged parser to produce recesses with a wide variety of shapes.*

There was a choice of a wide range of materials for the coverings. The selected material would first be filed to shape, using the boring plate as a pattern. The cutler might embellish the coverings by inletting a small metal escutcheon and to perform this operation he had a highly ingenious device the *two-legged* or *shielding parser*. With this tool the cutler could drill a hole of almost any shape he wished. The shielding parser resembled the ordinary parser but had, as its name implies, two 'legs' instead of the one. The ends were not pointed but were flattened out and had a step cut in them. The shielding parser was used in a similar fashion to the boring parser but in conjunction with a *shielding plate*, a hardened steel plate pierced with a hole of the desired shape. The material to be cut and the shielding plate were clamped together in the vice. The lightly sprung legs of the parser were brought together and the tips inserted into the hole of the shielding plate. Vigorous use of the boring stick caused the legs to rotate but their spring caused them to follow the outline of the hole in the plate. At the same time the cutting edges were scraping away the material behind the plate and were prevented from going right through by the shoulders on the legs coming into contact with its face. The result was a perfectly shaped recess in a very short time.

Any filed decoration to the backs of the blades or spring was then carried out to give the knife what is known as a *worked back* and the knife was then ready for final assembly. The escutcheons were pinned into their recess in the coverings, the coverings were pinned to the webs and the blades and springs riveted into position. Following assembly the knife was glazed and buffed all over to give the ultimate fine finish.

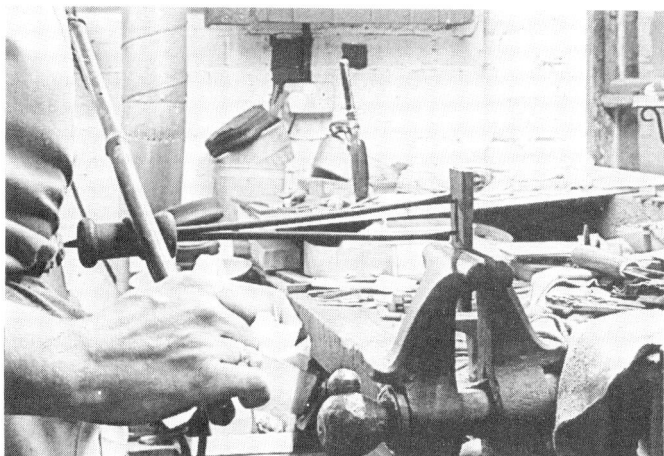

LEFT: The shielding parser being used by Graham Clayton, a spring-knife cutler, who has his workshop at the Kelham Island Industrial Museum, Sheffield.

RIGHT: Close-up of the shielding parser in use, showing how the tips of each leg are located within the hole of the shielding plate.

BELOW: The products and craftsmanship of Graham Clayton, a present-day spring-knife cutler.

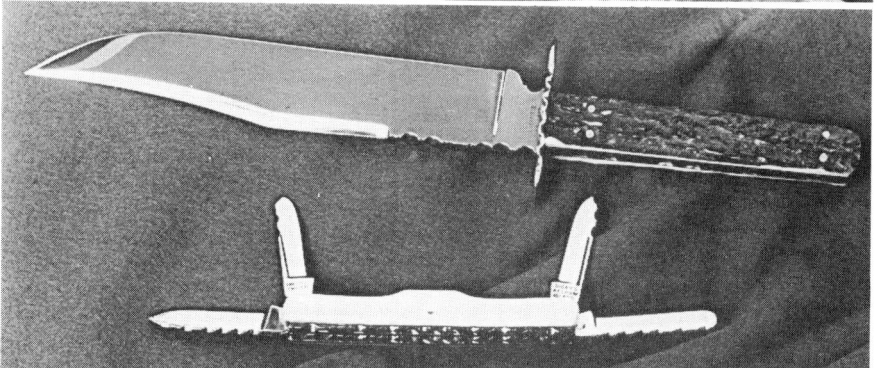

The razor grinder's 'hull' as depicted in the Illustrated London News in January 1866. Note the box-shaped structures, some fitted with a funnel-shaped top, intended to depict a rudimentary dust extraction system where dry grinding was in operation.

WORKING CONDITIONS

The rise of the wealthy factors and cutlery masters in the eighteenth century was the beginning of class distinction within the industry. These men gradually gained control of the Cutlers' Company in Sheffield and the interests of the working craftsmen, the main reason for establishing the company in the first place, were neglected. The craftsmen had, therefore, to find other means of protecting themselves and in the second half of the eighteenth century trades unions grew within the industry. Each specialist branch of the industry had its own union or trade society which fought for its members on such basic issues as piecework prices. When in 1787, for instance, the Sheffield Master Cutler had the idea of counting thirteen to the dozen, a blatant attempt to reduce piece-work prices, it provoked the first re-corded strike in the industry. It was also the theme of a cutting popular song by William Mather. The chorus gives some idea of the virulence of his attack upon the Master Cutler:

'And may the odd knife his great carcass
  dissect:
Lay open his vitals for men to inspect:
A heart full as black as the infernal gulf
In that greedy, blood sucking, bone
  scraping wolf.'

This was only one of many occasions on which the unions did battle not only with the masters but also with the law, for the mere existence of a union, in whatever guise, was illegal until the Trade Union Acts of 1871. Despite the justice of such causes the unions were to bring themselves notoriety in what became known as the Sheffield Outrages in the nineteenth century. Most unions had at first adopted

30

the rules and regulations which had originally protected the craftsmen under the auspices of the Cutlers' Company. As their power grew, however, some, particularly various grinders' unions, enforced their authority with a ruthlessness that amounted to terrorism, directed both at members who did not comply with the regulations and at employers who opposed the unions. They began simply by destroying or removing offenders' tools and equipment, known as *rattening*, a course of action which had its origins in the early guild systems, but some took matters to extremes. Assassinations were threatened and attempted. Some were even successful. Factories where mostly non-union workers were employed were liable to being blown up by gunpowder, as were some private homes. Despite the offer of substantial rewards few of the culprits were brought to trial and even fewer convicted. Matters became so serious that a government commission was set up in 1867 to investigate it, armed with unprecedented special powers to grant immunity to perpetrators who willingly gave evidence. The commission vindicated trade unionism in Sheffield, finding that most of these acts of violence were the work of a few clever and unscrupulous men and were abhorrent to the majority.

One of the occupational hazards faced by the grinders, the danger of bursting grindstones, has already been mentioned. But, for many grinders, a far greater hazard was the almost invisible dust produced in the grinding and glazing processes. Attacked by this dust from the day they began work, they would ultimately die of its effects. In the early days of the industry the grindstones were powered by waterwheels and the rivers of Sheffield abounded with such workshops or 'wheels'. With the introduction of the steam engine in the late eighteenth century large steam-powered grinding workshops *(steam wheels)* began to be built in the town itself. For the grinders it was a catastrophic change. They could no longer refresh themselves with clean country air between bouts of working while they waited for enough water to drive the wheel again or for it to be unlocked from the ice of winter. The steam engine could work all day, every day, regardless of the season. The grinders were crowded into poorly lit, badly ventilated workshops without respite for hours on end, and their lungs were filled with the dust of steel and sandstone created by their labours. It set like concrete in their lungs, making breathing agony. Known by a variety of names — grinder's lung, grinder's asthma, grinder's rot — the disease caused a slow and painful wasting away to be relieved only by death. Few grinders reached the age of thirty.

The craftsmen who suffered least from this affliction were the table-blade grinders, who used the wet grinding process in which no dust could be formed. The adoption of wet grinding by the pen and pocket blade grinders in the 1840s did much to alleviate the problem for them also but forks and razors continued to be ground dry. As early as 1823 attempts were made to try and eliminate the problem but some, like the Grinders' Life Preserver consisting of a magnet suspended under the nose like a magnetic moustache to trap particles of steel, were well intentioned but fanciful. In the following year the problem was attacked by Dr Knight of Sheffield, in conjunction with the London Society for Bettering the Conditions of the Poor, who offered a prize for the most effective means of prevention. The result was the extraction fan, but its adoption in the industry was resisted by factory owners because of the cost of installation. Twenty years later another Sheffield doctor, Calvert Holland, author of *The Mortality, Sufferings and Diseases of Grinders*, began a vigorous campaign to get the fan adopted, again to no avail. It was only with the extensions of the Factories Acts to cover the cutlery industry, beginning in 1867, that the use of the extraction fan became compulsory for all dry grinding and glazing processes. The risk of silicosis was not finally removed until the early twentieth century with the introduction of emery grindstones by George Jowitt of Sheffield.

FURTHER READING

Dyson, B. Ronald. *A Glossary of Old Sheffield Trade Words and Dialect.* Society for the Preservation of Old Sheffield Tools, Sheffield, 1936. An invaluable compendium of the terminology of the industry.

Flather, David. *Old Sheffield Craftsmen — Their Tools and Workshops.* Society for the Preservation of Old Sheffield Tools, Sheffield, 1934. Gives a valuable insight into some of the manufacturing processes.

Hayton, Dudley. *The Worshipful Company of Cutlers of London — A Brief History.* Cutlers' Hall, London, 1956, reprinted 1980. Contains some interesting points on the early trade.

Himsworth, J. B. *The Story of Cutlery.* Ernest Benn (for *the Hardware Trades Journal*), London, 1953. A valuable history of the industry and the products.

Lloyd, G. I. H. *The Cutlery Trades.* Longmans Green, London, 1913. Reprinted by Frank Cass, London, 1968. A superb study of the industry from the economic, social and organisational point of view though it lacks detail on the manufacturing processes.

Pollard, Sidney. *A History of Labour in Sheffield.* Liverpool University Press, 1959. A very detailed study of the social and working conditions in Sheffield during, mainly, the period 1850-1939. It contains a wealth of references.

Turner, C. A. *A Sheffield Heritage — An Anthology of Photographs and Words of the Cutlery Craftsmen.* Sheffield Trades Historical Society and Sheffield University Division of Continuing Education, 1978. A useful record of craftsmen and their methods in more recent times.

PLACES TO VISIT

Collections of cutlery and displays illustrating the processes of its manufacture are mainly to be found in Sheffield. Intending visitors are advised to find out the opening times before making a special journey.

Abbeydale Industrial Hamlet, Abbeydale Road South, Sheffield S7 2QW. Telephone: Sheffield (0742) 367731. An early water-powered site, principally concerned with the manufacture of agricultural edge tools but including many of the features mentioned in this book. It houses one of the few, and the earliest, surviving crucible steelmaking furnaces in Britain.

Company of Cutlers in Hallamshire, Cutlers' Hall, Sheffield. Small but fine collections of cutlery. Access by special arrangement.

Kelham Island Industrial Museum, Alma Street, Sheffield S3 8RY. Telephone: Sheffield (0742) 722106. Displays relating to the history of the trade in outline and covering some of the manufacturing processes, including working craftsmen.

Sheffield City Museum, Weston Park, Sheffield S10 2TP. Telephone: Sheffield (0742) 727226. A fine collection of cutlery of all types, spanning several centuries to the present day.

Shepherd Wheel, Whiteley Wood, Hangingwater Road, Sheffield. Telephone: Sheffield (0742) 367731. An early water-powered cutlery grinding workshop.

Victoria and Albert Museum, Cromwell Road, South Kensington, London SW7 2RL. Telephone: 01-589 6371. Extensive displays with many fine examples of cutlery selected for their aesthetic quality and covering the period from the sixteenth century to the present day.